OUR
Little Nuns

cartoons by
Joe Lane

published by About Comics, Camarillo, California

Our Little Nuns
Originally published by *Extension Magazine*, 1954
About Comics edition published April, 2018

Customized editions available

Send all queries to *questions@aboutcomics.com*

"Sister!"

"*Most unusual . . . want shoes that fit!*"

"We need someone to play Santa, Sister, and we were wondering if . . ."

"Mom and Dad, I'd like you to meet Mother Superior."

"Hut—2—3—4—!"

"What will I do, Sister? This recipe calls for brandy!"

"Your policies sound wonderful, Mr. Williams, but the least of our worries are death benefits."

"And if I had my life to live over again, Sister, I'd still wanna be in your room."

"Let's just try this for size."

"Well, if it isn't Maggie O'Rourke! What've you been doing all these years?"

"Oh, it isn't too bad—but the roofs leak."

"And have you been a good little girl?"

"Sorry, Mr. Greely, but I won't be at the supermart this summer!"

"Just the facts, Kunnegunda—Just give me the facts!"

"In these circumstances, Sister, is it obligatory to say Grace Before Meals?"

"Isn't it terrible, Sister? You can't get a thing for five dollars any more."

"A dozen pipe cleaners, please."

"This beats battling that subway every day!"

"Just a second there!"

"But, Sister, we're supposed to help little old ladies across the street!"

"Sister, can you play Chopsticks?"

"Dig that design! Why, Mother, that's real cool!"

"Take us out on the road to St. Margaret's Convent, and when the meter reads thirty-five cents, we'll get out and walk the rest."

"Who stole the ding dong? Who stole the bell?"

"Send this to the grocer, the butcher and the coal man . . . 'I have your previous statements, and may I say we are making a novena to St. Joseph for funds? As soon as he answers our prayers, you will receive a check. Sincerely . . .'"

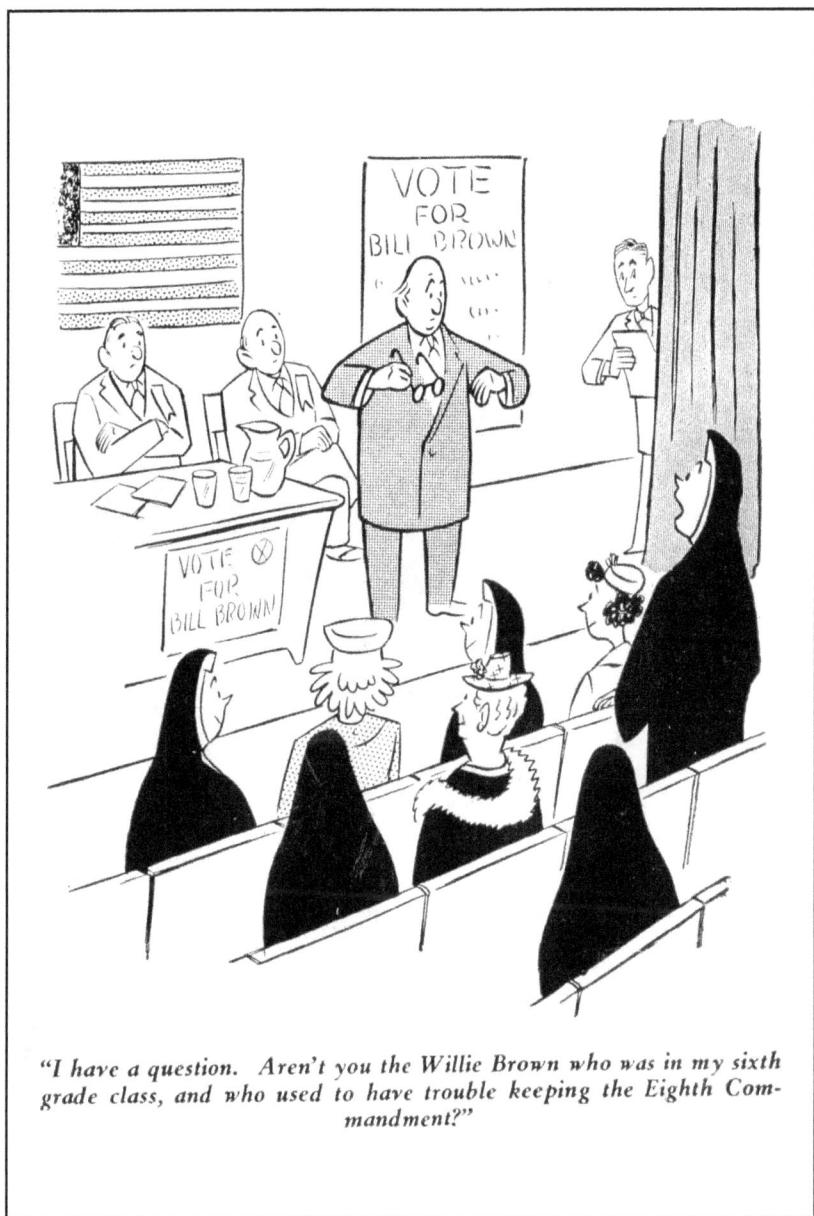

"I have a question. Aren't you the Willie Brown who was in my sixth grade class, and who used to have trouble keeping the Eighth Commandment?"

"No help from the audience, please!"

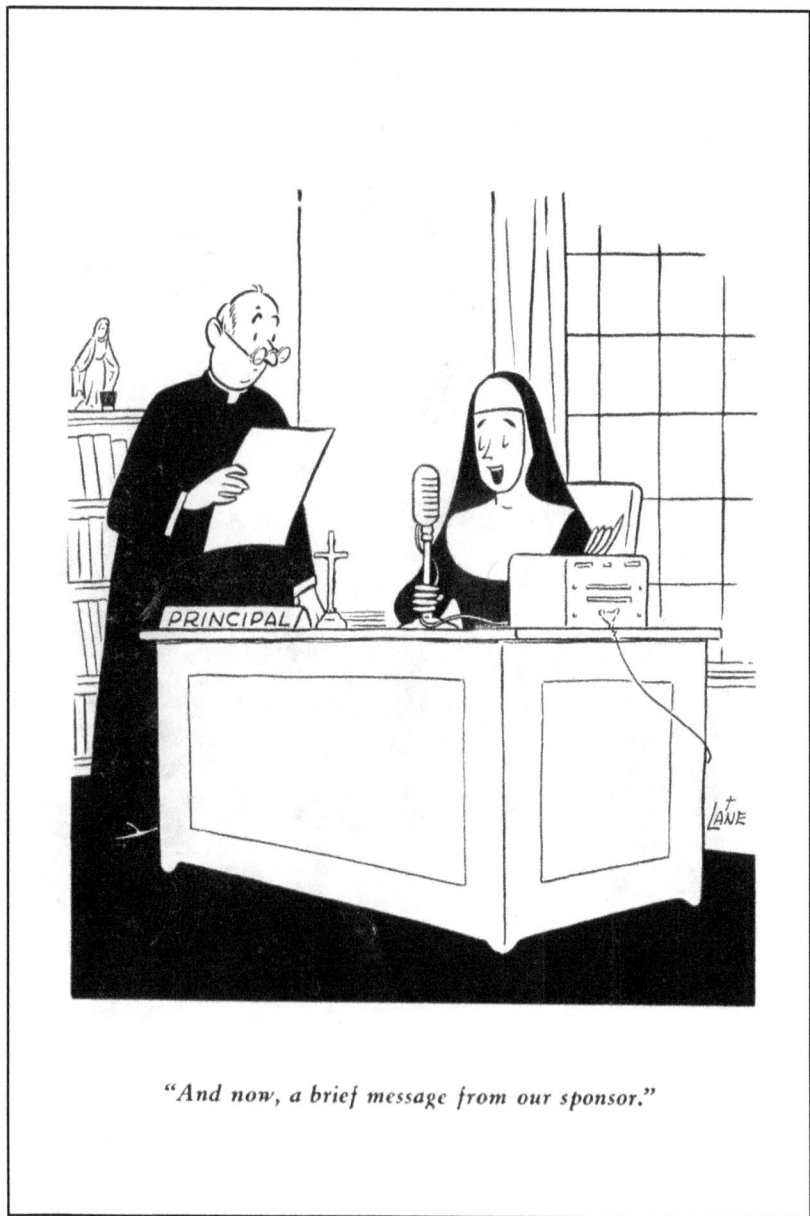

"And now, a brief message from our sponsor."

"*We don't have quite enough in cash, but we could remember you in our novenas!*"

"We'll start the day with the morning offering . . ."

"Nothing, thanks . . . just looking."

"Oh, Father—you're the answer to our prayers!"

"Dum de dum dum!"

"You gave me 3¢ too much change."

"Hmph!"

"*Reverend Father, Venerable Sister, distinguished guests, members of my class . . . I don't know the answer!*"

"The postulant's winter raiment in the novitiate differs somewhat from that of the outside world, Sister!"

"Sister will show you to your cells!"

"Cells???"

"That'll be $18.74, Sister."

". . . six hundred twenty-one, six hundred twenty-two, six hundred. . . ."

"Sister Mary Ignatia has one of the toughest classes in school!"

"Come on out, Sister, and get some suntan!"

"But, Sister, he's only going through a phase!"

"Happy birthday to you . . ."

"This is a good time to ask the pastor for a new blackboard."

"Now to find the motherhouse!"

"*I think it needs oil.*"

"And who left this in the bathtub?"

"$3.75 for just two of us . . . why, Sister, I can feed our whole convent for that!"

"I'm taking it in for the 1,000 mile check-up."

"*Today I'm introducing my class to the use of pens.*"

"No more fumbling . . . or, one of these days, Hennessy . . .
ONE OF THESE DAYS!"

"And when do we get to mold little minds and build strong characters
to face the vicissitudes of life?"

"Halo, everybody, halo . . ."

"Sh-boom! Sh-BOOM! Da-da-da-da-da-da-da-da-da-da-da-da!"

"I have to keep reminding myself they're children of God
and heirs of Heaven!"

"What discount can we get if you take out the cigarette lighter?"

"I must say, Sister, I have better deportment in my classroom!"

"It's such a beautiful day, Sister—Let's put the top down."

"All right, now, you men try and stop me!"

"Some nice furniture . . . for the convent, perhaps?"

Get all our little books of Joe Lane's little nuns

Our Little Nuns
More Little Nuns
Nuns So Lovable
Vale of Dears
Yes, Sister! No, Sister!

or get

The Big Book of Nun Cartoons
a lifetime supply all in one volume!

Look for them where you got this book,
or visit www.AboutComics.com

Classic Cartoon Collections!

www.ingramcontent.com/pod-product-compliance
Lightning Source LLC
Chambersburg PA
CBHW071845020426
42331CB00007B/1861